IMAGES
of America

ROUTE 66 IN OKLAHOMA

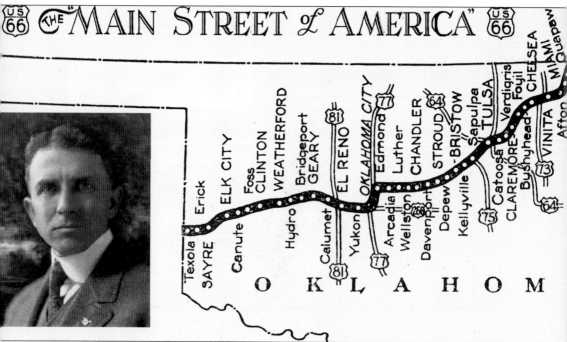

Cyrus Stevens Avery is known as the "Father of Route 66." The Tulsa businessman and county commissioner helped promote the Ozark Trails Route, which developed into Route 66. He made sure the route went through his hometown and past his gas station and tourist court. Avery became chairman of the Oklahoma Highway Commission and was appointed to the committee laying out the federal highway system. He proposed a highway from Chicago to Los Angeles along much of the Ozark Trails Route. After Route 66 was commissioned, Avery formed the US 66 Highway Association and coined the phrase "Main Street of America." In 2004, the 11th Street Bridge that carried Route 66 across the Arkansas River at Tulsa was renamed in his honor. In 2007, the City of Tulsa developed the Cyrus Avery Centennial Plaza at Southwest Boulevard and Riverside Drive. (Oklahoma Department of Transportation.)

ON THE COVER: By 1930, Phillips 66 had opened 6,000 outlets, including this one on Route 66 in Chandler. This station changed hands and brands over the years before closing in the 1980s. It was being completely restored in 2012. Pictured in this 1934 photograph are attendants Roger Hicks and Eul McMichael. (Keith Crall.)

IMAGES
of America

ROUTE 66 IN OKLAHOMA

Joe Sonderman and Jim Ross

ARCADIA
PUBLISHING

Published by Arcadia Publishing
Charleston, South Carolina

Printed in the United States of America

Library of Congress Control Number: 2011933825

For all general information, please contact Arcadia Publishing:
Telephone 843-853-2070
Fax 843-853-0044
E-mail sales@arcadiapublishing.com
For customer service and orders:
Toll-Free 1-888-313-2665

Visit us on the Internet at www.arcadiapublishing.com

In Memory of Bob Waldmire and Lucille Hamons

CONTENTS

ACKNOWLEDGMENTS

The authors wish to thank Shellee Graham, Jerry McClanahan, Laurel Kane, Mike Ward, Steve Rider, David Lopez and Gary Ray Howell of the Oklahoma Department of Transportation, Michael Wallis, Wanda Queenan, Kathy Anderson, Russell Olsen, and Vivian Payne.

Unless otherwise noted, all images appear courtesy of the authors.

INTRODUCTION

No state provides more "kicks on 66" than Oklahoma, the state with the most remaining miles of original route. Route 66 was born here, in the mind of Cyrus Avery. This is the birthplace of Will Rogers, Phillips 66 gasoline, and Andy Payne, winner of one of the most amazing athletic events of all time. Called the "Mother Road" by John Steinbeck in the *Grapes of Wrath*, Route 66 in Oklahoma will be forever linked with the desperate Dust Bowl days; however, it is also a symbol of freedom, opportunity, and adventure.

When Oklahoma joined the union in 1907, there were more miles of railway in the state than decent roads. Across the nation, private promoters were laying out a web of routes with fancy names like the Albert Pike Highway, the Jefferson Highway, the Kansas City–Tulsa Short Line, and the King of Trails. They were marked with symbols painted on phone poles, rocks, barns, or any handy surface. Motorists were often routed miles out of their way, past towns or businesses that paid subscriptions to the highway boosters.

In 1913, William Hope "Coin" Harvey formed the Ozark Trails Association (OTA) to promote a network of highways, initially intended to connect with his Monte Ne resort near Rogers, Arkansas. The main route linked St. Louis and Romeroville, New Mexico, by way of Oklahoma. The OTA erected tall concrete obelisks at key intersections, including one that still stands west of Stroud.

The vice president of the Ozark Trails Association, Cyrus Avery, operated the Old English Inn and Service Station on the eastern outskirts of Tulsa. He made sure the route went through his hometown and past his business. Avery was active in the Good Roads Movement and became chair of the Oklahoma State Highway Commission. In 1925, he was named to a committee of highway officials in charge of mapping out the proposed national highway system and creating a numbering scheme.

The federal committee assigned even numbers to the east-west routes, with the most important ending in zero. The Chicago-to-Los Angeles route was initially designated as US 60; however, the governor of Kentucky, William Fields, demanded the more important sounding number 60 for the route through his state. Avery and Missouri highway official B.H. Piepmeier refused, and a lengthy standoff ensued.

Finally, on April 30, 1926, Avery and his supporters met in Springfield, Missouri, to try and resolve the issue. At that meeting, Oklahoma's chief engineer John M. Page noticed that the catchy sounding 66 had not been assigned, and all agreed that it was an acceptable alternative. The new federal highway numbering system went into effect on November 11, 1926. At the time, less than one-fourth of the new Route 66 through Oklahoma was paved, and the pavement between Miami and Afton was just one lane wide.

In Eastern Oklahoma, the highway often followed township and section lines in a zig-zag pattern. In western Oklahoma at Bridgeport, it crossed the flood-prone Canadian River on a 1,000-foot-long suspension bridge built in 1921 by George Key, chairman of the state Democratic committee. Key raked in a steep $1 for each vehicle and $1.50 per truck, taking in about $200 per day. The Key Bridge was later bought by the state and made toll-free.

Avery and John T. Woodruff of Springfield, Missouri, invited businessmen and representatives of communities along the route to meet in Tulsa on February 4, 1927, forming the US 66 Highway Association. Avery suggested the group promote Route 66 as the "Main Street of America." The association saw a proposed transcontinental footrace as a chance to encourage awareness of the highway.

Sports promoter and showman C.C. "Cash and Carry" Pyle orchestrated the race, offering a first prize of $25,000. On March 4, 1928, a diverse group of 199 runners began a grueling journey from the Ascot Speedway in Los Angeles with Pyle's carnival-like sideshow. Just 80 runners remained when they left Oklahoma City, with local favorite Andy Payne of Foyil in the lead. Despite being slowed by huge crowds of well-wishers in his home state, Andy would go on to win, entering New York's Madison Square Garden hours ahead of the nearest contender. Pyle lost a pile of money, and Route 66 reaped a publicity bonanza.

The images of choking black dust clouds and overloaded jalopies are enduring symbols of Route 66 during the 1930s. But Steinbeck's "road of flight" also provided an economic lifeline for those who stayed to operate cafes, tourist courts, and gas stations. Government relief programs also put men to work improving the highway. Route 66 was fully paved across the state as of September 13, 1937, when Gov. Ernest W. Marland dedicated 14 miles of new pavement, replacing the one-lane "Sidewalk Highway" between Miami and Afton.

During World War II, leisure travel slowed to a trickle and the US 66 Highway Association faded away. The route did become a vital lifeline for the military, linking installations such as the Clinton Naval Air Station, Tinker Field in Oklahoma City, and the Douglas bomber factory in Tulsa. Another great migration took place as many headed west to seek work in the defense plants.

The golden years of Route 66 came after the war, when Nat King Cole recorded composer Bobby Troup's anthem to the highway, "Get Your Kicks on Route 66." GIs returned home, eager to take their families to the vacation wonderlands of the west. Legitimate roadside attractions with Western and Native American imagery and trinkets sprang up, such as the Buffalo Ranch in Afton, Chief Arrowood's in Catoosa, and Queenan's Trading Post in Elk City. There were also notorious tourist traps like the snake pits in western Oklahoma, some of which lured tourists into rigged games of chance.

In 1947, the US Highway 66 Association was reorganized, operated by Jack and Gladys Cutberth out of their home in Clinton. They promoted Route 66 as "the shortest, fastest year-'round best across the scenic West." The association could boast "800 miles of 4-lane highway" because a major transformation was slowly taking place. Increased traffic required bigger, faster, safer highways, and the end was soon in sight for major two-lane US highways like Route 66. Unfortunately, this would have dire consequences for many of those whose livelihoods depended on the highway.

Route 66 was evolving from the start. In 1932, a realignment turned Bridgeport into a ghost town. Wellston was bypassed when pavement arrived in 1933. In 1947, Gov. Roy J. Turner proposed a toll road to replace Route 66 between Oklahoma City and Tulsa. Despite opposition from communities along the route, the Turner Turnpike between Oklahoma City and Tulsa opened in 1953. The Will Rogers Turnpike opened from Tulsa to the Missouri line in 1957, and both became part of Interstate 44.

During the 1950s, Gov. Raymond Gary pushed to bring the current Route 66 in Western Oklahoma up to interstate standards. Interstate 40 was a safe distance south of Route 66 until just west of El Reno, though traffic wishing to avoid the congestion of motoring through Yukon and El Reno could join the interstate in Oklahoma City by 1967. Throughout the late 1950s and 1960s, Interstate 40 was completed piecemeal to the Texas line. However, no bypasses were opened around the cities of Weatherford, Clinton, Canute, Elk City, and Sayre until 1970. The final segment of Interstate 40, through Erick and Texola, opened in 1975.

Route 66 was decommissioned as a federal highway in 1985. Demoted to sections of State Highway 66, frontage roads, and county and city roads, Route 66 survives virtually intact. Route 66 is still a viable route for those who shun the turnpike and seek adventure. It waits at the next off-ramp.

One

OTTAWA AND
CRAIG COUNTIES

It was once common for businesses at state borders to be named Stateline Station, Stateline Tavern, or Stateline Trading Post, among other options. This Texaco station was located at the Oklahoma-Kansas state line. Eastbound motorists here immediately entered the city limits of Baxter Springs, Kansas. (Oklahoma Department of Transportation.)

Kansas Route 66 highway shields would be worth a substantial amount today but few still exist. Kansas has just 13 miles of Route 66, so very few signs were ever posted. Note the sign below the shield prohibiting tractors with lugged wheels. The studded wheels provided good traction in the field but played havoc with a paved surface. (Oklahoma Department of Transportation.)

Otttawa County was once the world's largest producer of lead and zinc. Route 66 travelers could tour some of the mines, including the Mary Jane, which boasted the "world's largest chat pile." The mines closed during the 1960s, leaving a legacy of health and environmental hazards. This chat (mining waste) pile is still there. (Steve Rider.)

The members of the Quapaw tribe were forced to turn their land in Arkansas over to the US government and were moved to a reservation in the Indian Territory, now northeastern Oklahoma. Indian Village at Quapaw lured Route 66 tourists with Native American dances, a buffalo herd, Texas longhorns, and a rodeo arena.

Route 66 runs down Main Street in Quapaw, shown here. On March 24, 1933, a big parade here marked the completion of 11 miles of pavement between Commerce, Oklahoma and Baxter Springs, Kansas. Quapaw chief Victor Griffin laid a commemorative zinc tablet in the middle of Main Street. Over 5,000 people, including Cyrus Avery, the Father of Route 66, attended the festivities. The tablet disappeared years later. (Steve Rider.)

Commerce is the hometown of baseball legend Mickey Mantle, and Route 66 in town is named Mickey Mantle Boulevard. This 1952 view looks north on Route 66 from First Street, past W.C. O'Brien's Court and the Glenbardo Court. The Glenbardo Court was originally O'Brien's camp. (Oklahoma Department of Transportation.)

D.E. Dion spent 33 years in the mines and lost his left eye before he quit and opened the Rock of Ages service station and rock shop in Commerce. During the Great Depression, about 25 stations around Miami sold specimens from natural caves found during mining for lead or zinc. Jim Mullen later operated the shop and station. (Steve Rider.)

Billed as "Miami's most recommended motor kourt," the Sooner State Kourt was described by AAA as "unusually nice." The 19-unit motel was built with the sandstone slabs so prevalent in the Ozarks. The Streamline Moderne sign featuring a Conestoga wagon was added about 1960. The Sooner State Kourt was torn down in 1981.

Art Tucker's Rainbow Cafe, "Cooled by Refrigeration," was located at 1214 North Main Street in Miami and was painted in a rainbow of colors. The Tucker family operated Tucker's Lunch in downtown Miami from 1928 to 1952. There were also Tucker's Lunch locations in Vinita, Picher, and Disney, Oklahoma.

The Ku-Ku chain once had over 200 locations, with buildings designed like giant cuckoo clocks. A bird at the top chimed every hour. Only one survives today, at 915 North Main Street in Miami. Eugene Waylan took over this location in 1973 and kept it going after the chain folded. The sign in front dates from 1965.

Miami, pronounced "My-AM-uh," was the first town chartered in the Indian Territory. It was originally known as Jimtown because four residents shared that name. Jim Palmer established the first post office and named it in honor of his wife, a Miami Indian. Miami grew dramatically after the discovery of lead and zinc in 1905.

George L. Coleman made a fortune in mining and built the Coleman Theatre as a gift to Miami. The Boller Bros. of Kansas City designed it in Spanish Colonial style, complete with hand carved gargoyles. The $590,000 theater opened on April 18, 1929. The Coleman family donated it to the city in 1989, and the theater was restored.

Ben Stanley's Cafe opened on February 8, 1947, in a prefabricated building made by the National Glass Manufacturing Company of Fort Smith, Arkansas. The building came complete with fixtures. Stanley served four terms as Ottawa County sheriff and was the US marshal for the Eastern District of Oklahoma during the Truman administration.

On March 1, 1922, 15.4 miles of roadway paved nine feet wide opened between Miami and Afton. Originally constructed as part of Oklahoma Route 7, it was hailed as a great achievement at the time. Under nicknames such as "Sidewalk Highway," "Scotch Pavement," and "Ribbon Road," it was bypassed in 1937. Two sections of this fragile roadway, parts of which have been covered with gravel, can still be driven with care.

The original Route 66 left Miami on South Main Street, crossing this beautiful concrete arch bridge over the Neosho River that connected to the "Sidewalk Highway." Route 66 was moved to a new steel truss bridge and a new alignment upstream in 1937. The old concrete arch bridge was later replaced with a nondescript span that still stands today.

Gov. Ernest W. Marland used a giant pair of scissors to cut the ribbon on September 13, 1937, opening the new Neosho River Bridge and new pavement between Miami and Afton. The new road replaced the infamous "Sidewalk Highway," and was the last portion of Route 66 in Oklahoma to be paved to standards. Despite a last-ditch effort by preservationists, this bridge was torn down in 1999. (Steve Rider.)

The Spanish Revival–style Riviera Courts opened on the new Route 66 south of Miami in 1937. The units are faced with oversized brick and separated by garages. The Riviera Courts became the Holiday Motel in the late 1950s. The building has been vacant since about 1978 and is listed in the National Register of Historic Places.

Russell and Aleene Kay opened the Buffalo Ranch Trading Post at the junction with US 59 on July 11, 1953. They started with seven bison. Betty Wheatley ran the adjacent Dairy Ranch for 42 years. The Buffalo Ranch closed after Aleene died. It was leveled in 1998. A few buffalo remain behind the convenience store constructed on the site.

Larue Olson and his trained 1,800-pound buffalo Pat performed at the Buffalo Ranch. Larue rode the "World's Only Trained Buffalo" in Pres. John F. Kennedy's inaugural parade and toured rodeos throughout the United States. Olson always said buffalos could be trained but not tamed, and Pat eventually killed him.

The Eagle D-X station opened in 1933, changed owners and brands over the years, and then was left vacant. Laurel Kane and her husband at the time, David, came from Connecticut in 2000 and began restoration. Afton Station is now a popular visitor's center featuring Laurel's extensive postcard collection and David's stable of rare Packards.

Afton was founded in 1886 and named for Afton Aires, the daughter of a railroad surveyor. The surveyor named his daughter after the Afton River in his native Scotland. The Palmer Hotel, visible at the far right, opened in 1911. Alvin and Lulu Maloney took over in 1952. The Palmer has been vacant since Lulu died in 1991.

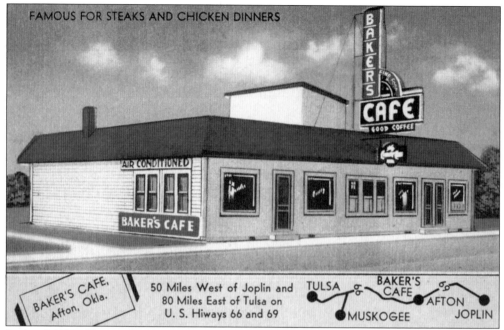

FAMOUS FOR STEAKS AND CHICKEN DINNERS

BAKER'S CAFE, Afton, Okla.

50 Miles West of Joplin and 80 Miles East of Tulsa on U. S. Hiways 66 and 69

TULSA — BAKER'S CAFE — AFTON
MUSKOGEE — JOPLIN

In April 1932, Clint and Lillie Baker took over a small barbeque restaurant on Main Street. It grew into Baker's Cafe, with seating for 120. During the Depression, Clint offered a meal and 50¢ to anyone who would work for an hour. The Bakers sold the cafe in 1947, and the building later became a daycare center.

Clint's Cafe

AFTON, OKLAHOMA

Clint Baker later opened Clint's Cafe. The sign blared that it was "Famous for Food." Clint's became the Davis Cafe in the 1950s. The building sat vacant for some time before becoming Linda McCloud's Route 66 Cafe, which burned in 2009. The building is now used by an auction service.

John Foley constructed the Avon Court on the west end of Afton in 1936. W.R. Trebilcock owned it from 1951 to 1955, when he sold it to Harry Glover. Glover sold it after the Will Rogers Turnpike opened in 1957. The ruins of the old court remain a symbol of the days when Afton bustled with Route 66 traffic. (Laurel Kane.)

In 1936, mail carrier Sullivan Johnson and his wife, Ureatha, opened the Acme Courts on the west end of Afton. They advertised, "A clean, comfortable place for you and your family. Our slogan—You must be satisfied." The station sold Conoco Bronz-z-z Gasoline. Just one crumbling unit remains today, with a newer building attached.

The sharp turn at "Deadman's Corner" between Afton and Vinita was replaced by a sweeping curve when Route 66 was paved in 1930. The space between the new curve and the old corner made a perfect spot for a roadside park, complete with tables and brick fireplaces for cooking or heat. No trace of this wayside stop remains. (Oklahoma Department of Transportation.)

Native American educator Agnes "Sunflower" Dill and her husband, Clarence "Buffalo" Dill, operated their trading post and museum nine miles east of Vinita from 1948 to 1965, when they moved to Isleta Pueblo in New Mexico. After Clarence died, Agnes became an activist for Native American women. She was one of the founding members of the North American Indian Women's Association, formed in 1971, and became the president of the organization in 1973. At age 97 in 2010, Agnes was awarded an honorary doctorate from the University of New Mexico.

The Lewis Motel in Vinita was across the street from Clanton's Cafe, the oldest continuously run family-owned restaurant on Oklahoma's Route 66. "Sweet Tater" Clanton opened the cafe in 1927. Marked by a simple "EAT" sign and famous for chicken-fried steak, Clanton's was rebuilt after a fire on December 25, 1997. The Lewis Motel was demolished in 2006.

When Route 66 was first commissioned, most hotels were designed to serve railroad travelers. The Hotel Vinita, at left, was constructed in 1930 and oriented to face Route 66. Mont Green originally owned the five-story Spanish Revival–style hotel. It was then operated by the Boone Hotel chain until 1969. The lower level now houses shops.

Vinita, the seat of Craig County, was originally known as Dowlingville. It was renamed in 1871 in honor of sculptress Vinnie Ream. She created statues of Abraham Lincoln and Sequoyah for the nation's capitol. The bus in this photograph is parked in front of C.J. Wright's Cafeteria. The site is now an auto dealership.

As the popularity of the Holiday Inn chain grew, several motels along Route 66 took the name Holiday. At the time this image was captured, Gene and Hazel Davis operated the Holiday Motel at 519 South Wilson Street. Note the similarity to the famous Holiday Inn sign and the big plastic globes around the pool. It became the Route 66 Inn at Vinita.

The Motel Vinita was constructed on shady grounds where the 1930s alignment of Route 66 curves to the west toward White Oak and Chelsea. The original 1926 alignment can be seen continuing south on Wilson Street to Euclid Street before turning west. Nick Douvas owned the 17-unit ranch-style motel, which became the Relax Inn.

Shell Camp is an example of the early tourist accommodations on Route 66. In 1932, the camp offered "36 individual cabins with private baths, gas heated and furnished with gas hot plates. City lights, water, and sewerage, general store and free ice water. Renting for $1, $1.50 with kitchenettes and linen furnished." A camping space cost 25¢.

Jim's Restaurant opened about 1948 on the curve at the south end of Vinita and was described by AAA as "a small restaurant serving good food." Jim's specialties included steaks, chicken, and Italian dishes. This structure no longer stands. A restaurant now occupies the site at 335 South Dwain Willis Avenue. (Route 66.)

The Quarter Horse Motel, located three miles west of Vinita, had 13 units for people and stables for horses. Their motto was, "We bed the man, park the trailer and barn the horse," and the motel advertised the "sweetest rest this side of heaven." The Quarter Horse Motel was owned and operated by Mr. and Mrs. Henry Wrage.

Two

Rogers County

From 1908 until 1940, Sears and Roebuck sold thousands of prefabricated homes by mail order and shipped the materials by rail. In 1913, Joseph Sterling Hogue of Chelsea assembled a Hamilton model, which sold for $1,600. The home, the only one of its kind west of the Mississippi, is located a block off Route 66.

The Chelsea Motel opened about 1936 on the paved alignment of Route 66 where it met the original 1926 route over First Street through Chelsea. Georgia Palen sold the property to Nellie Bly Parker in 1939. Ted and Mildred Noland took over in 1946 and erected the neon sign that still stands outside the motel, which closed about 1976.

Ed Galloway's Totem Pole Park is a short detour off Route 66, east of Foyil. The wood carver and industrial arts teacher retired to this farm in 1937 and began building totem poles, including the largest in the world. Plastering mortar over a framework of steel and wire, the elaborate poles took Galloway 11 years to finish.

Ed Galloway made almost 400 hand-carved fiddles, which he displayed in the 11-sided Fiddle House at Totem Pole Park. Galloway died in 1962, and thieves made off with most of the fiddles. The park deteriorated until the Kansas Grassroots Art Association and the Rogers County Historical Society began restoration in 1983.

Andy Payne, a part Cherokee from Foyil, won the 1928 Bunion Derby. The epic transcontinental footrace made Route 66 front-page news. In Andy's home state, huge crowds like this one in El Reno cheered and sometimes hampered his progress. As Andy (no. 43 at left) arrived in Claremore on April 17, Will Rogers joked he was "being replaced as Oklahoma's favorite son." (El Reno Carnegie Library.)

Andy Payne ran 3,422 miles in 573 hours, 40 minutes, and 13 seconds to win the Bunion Derby. The $25,000 first prize helped pay off the mortgage on his parent's farm, and Payne married his former high school teacher Vivian Shaddox. Andy served as clerk of the Oklahoma Supreme Court and died in 1977. Route 66 in Foyil is now named Andy Payne Boulevard, where a statue honors his superhuman feat. (El Reno Carnegie Library.)

Many area children took swimming lessons in the pool at the Cozy Court on the north side of Claremore, owned by Mr. and Mrs. S.M. Miller. The attached garages were later connected, and it became the 19-unit Cozy Motel and Trailer Park. The driveway of the motel, later owned by R.E. Riley, was lined with covered wagons and teepees.

In addition to Will Rogers, Claremore is also the hometown of singer Patti Page and playwright Rollie Lynn Riggs. Riggs wrote *Green Grow the Lilacs*, the basis for the musical *Oklahoma*. Claremore was once famous as "Radium Town," with bathhouses offering a soak in the foul-smelling mineral water that was touted as having healing qualities. (Oklahoma Department of Transportation.)

Jack Sibley quit his job as state tax commissioner in 1938 and opened El Sueno, or "the Dream," the first motel on Route 66 in Claremore. Sibley modeled El Sueno after the Alamo Plaza chain motels and made his home on the second floor. The 18-unit motel later became the Adobe Village Apartments.

Louis Abraham, Walter Krumrei, and Morton Harrison built the Will Rogers Hotel, dedicated on February 7, 1930. Will Rogers said, "I was more proud to see my name in electric lights in my old home town and on an institution built for service to the public than I ever was on the biggest theatre on Broadway." The hotel, which featured radium baths on the top floor, closed in 1991. It was restored in 1997 and now houses apartments for seniors.

John Monroe Davis was given his first gun at the age of seven and went on to gather the world's largest private individual collection. He displayed them on the walls of his Hotel Mason in Claremore. The collection of over 20,000 weapons was leased to the state for $1 in 1965. The guns are now displayed at the J.M. Davis Arms and Historical Museum a few blocks away.

Beloved comedian and philosopher Will Rogers and famed Oklahoma aviator Wiley Post died when their plane crashed in Alaska on August 15, 1935. Tulsa attorney J.B. Underwood quickly launched a movement to name Route 66 the Will Rogers Highway. The US 66 Highway Association adopted the name in December 1935. The reorganized association abandoned it in 1947. (Oklahoma Department of Transportation.)

Will Rogers purchased 21 acres overlooking the Tiawah Valley in 1911, planning to retire there. The family donated the land after his death, and the state erected the memorial museum, dedicated on the 58th anniversary of his birth on November 4, 1938. John Duncan Forsythe of Tulsa designed the original structure of native stone.

A sunken garden on the museum grounds contains the tomb of Will Rogers, his wife, Betty, and members of his immediate family. Will was originally buried in California, and his body was brought here on May 22, 1944. A statue of Will atop his favorite horse, Soapsuds, was erected in 1950. Electra Waggoner designed the statue.

Kurl's Kourt, located at the south end of Claremore, was owned and operated by Joseph and Alice Boucher and, later, by Mr. and Mrs. Willie Ramm. The Ramms expanded it into the Lucky Motel, which was later operated by Bernice Green. The Jack Kissee Ford dealership was built on this site.

Red and Sally Oats owned the Round-Up Motel. They welcomed pets and offered Western-style furnishings, a free TV in every room, complimentary baby beds, and morning coffee free of charge. The Round-Up Motel was demolished in 2001, and the sign featuring a cowboy blowing smoke rings with his cigarette ended up in a private collection.

WILL ROGERS COURT – HIGHWAY 66, 1 MILE SOUTH CLAREMORE, OKLA.

The Will Rogers Court in Claremore became the Will Rogers Motor Court, operated by William and Opal Gaddis. The motor court was extensively remodeled to resemble a chalet in 1963. Another expansion took place in 2001, and it is now the Will Rogers Magnuson Hotel, 920 South Lynn Riggs Boulevard.

Catoosa Trailer Sales
U. S. Hwy. 66
Catoosa, Okla.

The name Catoosa comes from the Cherokee word *Catoos*, which means "new settlement place." It was a wild place during the cattle drive days. Today, it is the furthest inland port in the United States that remains ice-free year round. The 445-mile McClellan-Kerr Arkansas River Navigation System connects Catoosa to the Arkansas and Mississippi Rivers. Don Eigle operated Catoosa Trailer Sales on Route 66.

These nearly identical bridges spanning the natural channel of the Verdigris River were called "Felix" and "Oscar" by locals. The westbound span opened in 1936, and the eastbound bridge was built in 1957. Sadly, the westbound span was replaced in 2011. Two sections of the old bridge are now part of the entrance to the nearby Molly's Landing Restaurant.

Acoma tribesman Wolf Robe Hunt's original trading post was located in Tulsa. In 1952, he partnered with his brother-in-law Hugh Davis to open the Catoosa Trading Post next to the Davis property. It later became the Arrowood Trading Post, which closed in the 1990s. The building became an auto repair shop, but the trading post markings remain. (Oklahoma Historical Society.)

Hugh Davis ran the Mohawk Park Zoo for 38 years before retiring. His wife, Zelta, was also a fearless animal handler who convinced him to open the Catoosa Alligator Ranch about 1967. It grew into Nature's Acres, a park complete with gators, snakes, a prairie dog town, and a kid-sized ark populated with painted cutout animals. Hugh and his grandson John Davis are shown here at the ARK, which stood for Animal Reptile Kingdom. (The Davis/Belt family.)

Zelta Davis is shown with Betty, a gator that once latched onto her arm and dragged her into the water. Zelta punched her in the snout to escape. In 1970, Hugh Davis and his friend Harold Thomas began building an 80-foot-long concrete whale with a slide and diving board. It cost $1,910.24 and took 126 sacks of concrete to build the Blue Whale, which Hugh presented to Zelta on their anniversary.

The Blue Whale became so popular that Hugh and Zelta closed Natures Acres to focus on the swimming hole. The grinning leviathan deteriorated after the attraction closed in 1988 but was restored in 1997. The Blue Whale is now owned by Dee Dee (Davis) Belt and her husband, Dick. Sons John and Paul help maintain one of the most beloved icons on Route 66. (The Davis/Belt family.)

Three

TULSA COUNTY

Toby's Beauty Rest Courts offered attractive wood framed cabins that rented for $3 per night at the time this view was captured. The cottages were air conditioned and offered locked garages and Beautyrest mattresses. An addition has been constructed onto the home, but the cabins at 13330 East 11th Street were still standing in 2011.

A TERMINAL BUILDING AND FILLING STATION ISLAND OF PIERCE PENNANT TERMINALS SYSTEM
FACILITIES INCLUDE: 154-PERSON RESTAURANT, WOMEN'S REST ROOM, SODA AND SANDWICH LOBBY
EMERGENCY HOSPITAL

NEAR COLUMBIA, MO.	NEAR MIAMI, OKLA.	NEAR TULSA, OKLA.
(ON U. S. HIGHWAY 40)	(ON U. S. HIGHWAY 66)	(ON U. S. HIGHWAY 66)

In the late 1920s when most roadside accommodations were rudimentary, Henry Clay Pierce of the Pierce Pennant Petroleum Company envisioned a chain of lavish hotels and facilities for motorists every 125 miles in the Missouri Ozarks and Oklahoma. Six were completed, including this one at 12100 East 11th Street in Tulsa. It later became the Bates Tourist Hotel, which was abandoned for several years and then demolished.

AAA said the Saratoga Motor Hotel at 10117 East 11th Street offered "large, tastefully appointed units in a very good motel." The 85-unit Saratoga advertised "circulating ice water, 21-inch console TV," and "continuous hi-fi music." It is now America's Value Inn, and the distinctively shaped sign is still in use.

Route 66 originally entered Tulsa via 193rd Avenue, 11th Street, Mingo Road, Admiral Place, Lewis Avenue, and Second Street. Cyrus Avery, the Father of Route 66, ran this station, tourist court, and restaurant at Mingo Road and Admiral Place. Route 66 was rerouted to stay on 11th Street west from Mingo Road in 1932, and Avery's complex was torn down in 1943 for construction of the traffic circle. (Mike Ward.)

The Admiral Twin Drive-In was originally the Modernaire. It opened on May 24, 1951, screening *Oh Susanna*, starring Forrest Tucker. The name was changed when a second screen was added in 1952. The Admiral Twin was featured in the 1983 movie *The Outsiders* and bounced back from a devastating fire in September 2010. (Beryl Ford Collection/Rotary Club of Tulsa, Tulsa City-County Library, Tulsa Historical Society.)

This view of the Oasis Motel at 9303 East 11th Street shows the original sign, erected when the motel was constructed in 1953. It was replaced by an equally attractive sign about 1960. Mr. and Mrs. C.E. Walker offered free coffee at all times and a "sitter list." The Oasis is still in business today and the c. 1960 sign is still there.

James Norcom owned several motels in Tulsa, including the Manor Motel. It opened in 1958 at the intersection of Route 66 and Oklahoma Route 11 (now Memorial Drive). The 22-unit motel had wood-burning fireplaces, and the attached stone-covered ranch-style cabins resembled the popular modern home designs of the era.

The US 66 Cafe was located on the northwest corner of East 11th Street and Memorial Drive. It advertised, "Midway between New York and Los Angeles where the cross country travelers meet and eat. Remember to Get Your Kicks on 66 and don't fail to stop at our completely air conditioned coffee shop and dining room, seats 135."

Tulsa Ranch-O-Tel. 7930 E. 11th St., Tulsa, Okla.

Recommended by AAA, the Tulsa Ranch-O-Tel was located at 7930 East 11th Street, just west of Memorial Drive. It was advertised as one of Tulsa's newest and finest motels with a convenient cafe, "Where the West Begins. The complex offered deluxe rooms, featuring Western furnishings and "Safe-Air heating."

Architect William Henry Ryan's design for the Rose Bowl Lanes was inspired by the strong domed concrete bomb shelters he saw in Germany during World War II. Featured in the movie *UHF*, the bowling alley opened in 1962 and closed in 2005. After a few arson attempts, it reopened as the Rose Bowl Event Center in 2007.

Parkey's Restaurant at 6327 East 11th Street was open around the clock, advertising "Fine Food—Friendly Service—Tourists Welcome" and inviting diners to "come as you are." The restaurant closed in the mid-1970s, and the building housed a shooting range followed by a series of bars and a pool hall before being demolished in 2010.

The Sheridan Hills Motel, located at 6302 East 11th Street, was notable for its heated swimming pool enclosed with colorful glass, as shown in this view. AAA described the Sheridan Hills as "attractively decorated, with nicely furnished rooms in a brick motel with air conditioning." It is now the Super 11 Inn.

45 COTTAGES   COOK'S COURT   TULSA OKLA.
TRAV-O-TEL

Cook's Court at 5946 East 11th Street advertised it was "Tulsa's Largest." Owner E.L. "Gene" Roop offered "38 modern units, innerspring mattresses, steam or gas heat, air-cooled, kitchenettes, radios, moderate priced. Patronage appreciated and service with a smile." Paintmaster Collision Center is located here today.

The 36-unit Flamingo Motel at 5915 East 11th Street was a very nice and colorful brick motel with large, inviting rooms. It advertised "a first class motel" with "lots of hospitality," just 10 minutes from downtown and featuring a new restaurant serving fine food one block away. It still stands today as the Western Inn.

"Tulsa's Most Popular," the Tulsa Motel at 5715 East 11th Street opened in 1941 and featured nicely landscaped grounds. It originally had 20 cottages that were entered from the garages to ensure privacy and advertised Goodyear air foam mattresses. It was expanded to 72 units and then 82. The site is a car lot today.

The Will Rogers Motor Court opened in 1941 at 5737 East 11th Street. Paul and Dora Johnson took over in 1947, adding the classic neon sign with a rearing horse and its rider in 1951. The motor court had 36 units, and a swimming pool was added in 1958. McCollum's Restaurant next door was a popular spot, but both are now gone. (Mike Ward.)

Whitt's Motel was a comfortable place, advertising "indirect lighting, which insures comfort, relaxation for guests," as well as "sound-proofed rooms, easy chairs, excellent beds and everything for your comfort." It later became the Bel-Air Motel, and the site is now a parking lot. (Beryl Ford Collection/Rotary Club of Tulsa, Tulsa City-County Library, Tulsa Historical Society.)

The Desert Hills Motel opened in 1957 with the rooms built at angles. The layout allowed more large rooms to be built on the small lot at 5220 East 11th Street. The 50-unit Desert Hills fell into disrepair in the 1970s, but Jack Patel renovated the property after he took over in 1996. The motel is still in business today.

In 1948, Milton and Lemuel Stroud, founders of the Park Plaza Courts motel chain, opened the Golden Drumstick in the former Casa del Club at East 11th Street and Yale Avenue. Bob Latting, "Tulsa's First TV Personality," was one of the owners. It later became a health food restaurant called the Middle Path, and the site is now a convenience store.

In 1934, Beatrice Foods erected a large neon sign advertising Meadow Gold milk at 11th Street and Lewis Avenue. The building was demolished in 2004, but the sign was saved and restored with help from the Tulsa Foundation for Architecture and the National Park Service. In 2009, it was placed atop a pavilion near 11th Street and Quaker Avenue. (Beryl Ford Collection/Rotary Club of Tulsa, Tulsa City-County Library, Tulsa Historical Society.)

Harry H. Mahler designed the Tulsa Monument Building, constructed in 1936. The streamline Art Deco–style structure strongly resembles a monument. It now houses Banner Monument, and is listed in the National Register of Historic Places.

Leroy Borden and his brother Richard opened their first restaurant in 1935. They eventually had seven restaurants and cafeterias. The last one closed in 1985. Borden's, located at 2615 East 11th Street, advertised "complete breakfast service" with "truly delicious coffee that will highlight any meal." (Beryl Ford Collection/Rotary Club of Tulsa, Tulsa City-County Library, Tulsa Historical Society.)

Tulsa is known for Art Deco buildings like the Warehouse Market, designed by B. Gaylord Noftsger and opened in 1929. In 1993, Home Depot planned to raze it for parking, but a public outcry saved the facade and the terra cotta–adorned tower. Only the back of the structure was removed. (Beryl Ford Collection/Rotary Club of Tulsa, Tulsa City-County Library, Tulsa Historical Society.)

The Boston Avenue United Methodist Church, just off Route 66, is Tulsa's Art Deco gem. University of Tulsa art department founder Adah Robinson collaborated with former student Bruce Goff on the design featuring a 225-foot-tall tower. The $1.25 million church opened on June 9, 1929. Its exterior is decorated with terra cotta sculptures by Robert Garrison, who also was once a student of Adah Robinson's.

You'll come to Bishop's

Bishop's Driv - Inn

You'll return to Bishop's

10th and Boston

SEATING CAPACITY 156
ON HIGHWAYS 66 AND 44

TULSA, OKLAHOMA

William Wallace Bishop owned several eateries in Tulsa and later operated restaurants from Oklahoma City to Hollywood. Bishop's Driv-Inn at 10th Street and Boston Avenue opened in 1938 but closed in 1942 due to wartime shortages. The building housed a depot for transporting workers to manufacturing plants and later became the Capps Restaurant. The site is now a parking lot.

The Chastain Oil Company's Blue Dome Station opened in 1925. Designers Lawrence Blue and Fred Knoblock were inspired by the Hagia Sophia church in Istanbul, Turkey. The manager lived in the dome, and the station was the first in Tulsa to offer amenities such as a car wash and free air. It closed in the 1940s. Restored by developer Michael Sager, it is now the heart of the Blue Dome District, a center of Tulsa's nightlife. (Beryl Ford Collection/Rotary Club of Tulsa, Tulsa City-County Library and Tulsa Historical Society.)

John and Cass Mayo's hotel, the grandest in Tulsa, opened in 1925. It hosted notables such as Harry Truman, John F. Kennedy, Charles Lindbergh, and Elvis Presley. It was also the home of oilman John Paul Getty. The Mayo closed in 1981 and was abandoned for 20 years before it was saved by the Snyder family. It reopened in 2009 after a $40 million renovation.

Tulsa was settled between 1828 and 1836 by Creek Indians driven from their Alabama homes by the US government. The Creek named the settlement Tulasi, which means "old town." In 1882, the settlement became known as "Tulsey Town," and became the terminus of the St. Louis and San Francisco, or "Frisco" Railroad. The discovery of Oil at Red Fork in 1901 triggered a boom that established Tulsa as the "Oil Capital of the World."

The 11th Street Bridge over the Arkansas River, completed in 1917, has 18 concrete spans and is 1,470 feet long. As a county commissioner, Cyrus Avery was involved in its construction, and the bridge was a factor in determining the path of Route 66. It closed in 1980. The bridge was renamed in honor of Cyrus Avery in 2004.

53

The Cyrus Avery Centennial Plaza, at the east end of the 11th Street Bridge, was dedicated in 2008. The centerpiece will be a sculpture titled "East Meets West," created by Robert Summers. The work depicts the Avery family in a Model T meeting a startled horse. Future plans for the plaza also include an interpretive center and archives.

Offering a "Chicken Box to Go" for 66¢, 66 Chicken and Steaks did all it could to capitalize on its Mother Road location. At the time, the roadway in West Tulsa was named South Quanah Avenue and carried US 66 and US 75. Quanah Avenue south of the Arkansas River became Southwest Boulevard in the 1950s.

This photograph was taken in February 1950, just after the old two-lane Route 66 through West Tulsa had been upgraded to four lanes. The view faces east on Southwest Boulevard/Route 66 from 25th Street. Today, no trace remains of the structures shown in this photograph. (Oklahoma Department of Transportation.)

Milton and Lemuel Stroud built the first Park Plaza Courts at Quanah Avenue and 35th Street in 1942. They had permission to adopt the design used by the Alamo Plaza chain. The Park-Plaza chain grew to include six locations. Four were spaced a day's drive apart along Route 66 at St. Louis, Tulsa, Amarillo, and Flagstaff. The Tulsa location was demolished in 1988.

The 66 Motel was originally the El Reposo Tourist Camp, built by Isaac Burnaman about 1933. It had 17 small concrete block and stucco units that were entered from the garages to ensure privacy. Noma and Ken Undernehr, shown here, operated the 66 Motel from 1967 into the 1980s. The motel was torn down in 2000. (Shellee Graham.)

Bell gas was a popular brand of gasoline during the heyday of Route 66. This station was in West Tulsa, within walking distance of the iconic 66 Motel in one direction and the Shady Rest Court in the other, both of which have been destroyed. The crumbling ruin of the station still stands. (Oklahoma Department of Transportation.)

Tulsa plumbing inspector Maurice Colpitts hired a contractor to build the Shady Rest Tourist Court in 1936. He may have used a design published in *Popular Mechanics* magazine for the 10-foot by 12-foot cabins. The Shady Rest deteriorated badly late in its life, with rooms renting for $65 per week. It was demolished in 2005.

This 1949 view of Route 66 in Red Fork looks east from near today's Interstate 44 and West 41st Street. The first oil well in Tulsa County was completed in Red Fork on June 25, 1901. Within a few months, the population grew from about 75 to 1,500. Red Fork was annexed into the City of Tulsa in October 1927. The buildings on the right remain today. (Oklahoma Department of Transportation.)

A Route 66 bypass was established along Skelly Drive in 1951. After improvements were completed in 1959, Skelly was designated as Interstate 44 and US 66. Bob and Betty Saxby operated the Oil Capital Motel "at the sign of the pumping oil well," 802 West Skelly. It later became the Budget Inn.

This postcard for the Frontier Motel, 5510 West Skelly Drive, advertised that the rooms were equipped with the famous "Magic Finger" massaging beds. Many motel beds were equipped with the vibrating units until patrons began breaking into the coin boxes. The Frontier later became the Crystal Motel.

West of Tulsa, Route 66 originally followed Southwest Boulevard and Sapulpa Road. The route was shifted to today's State Highway 66 in 1951. In 1950, the Western Capri Motel opened at 5320 Sapulpa Road, now West Skelly Drive. The motel was still standing in 2011, but the beautiful sign was sent to a scrap dealer and destroyed in 2006.

The Sands Motor Hotel opened in 1957 at 51st Street and Sapulpa Road, now West Skelly Drive. The Sands advertised a location one mile from the Turner Turnpike Gate, as well as "continuous music at all times." The motel later became the American Value Inn and Suites, and the restaurant became a strip club.

The attractive Town and Country Motor Hotel, 5600 New Sapulpa Road, (now West Skelly Drive) had a fine restaurant. It later became the Gateway Motor Hotel. The Gateway is one of a string of motels in this stretch that have fallen on hard times. (Beryl Ford Collection/Rotary Club of Tulsa, Tulsa City-County Library, Tulsa Historical Society.)

Four

CREEK AND LINCOLN COUNTIES

As traffic increased on Route 66 after World War II, Gov. Roy J. Turner worked with lawmakers to establish the Oklahoma Turnpike Authority; however, legal challenges delayed the ground breaking until December 1950. The former governor cut the ribbon when the Turner Turnpike between Tulsa and Oklahoma City opened on May 16, 1953. The Will Rogers Turnpike, connecting Tulsa and the Missouri line and bypassing all of Route 66 in Kansas, opened in 1957. (Oklahoma Department of Transportation.)

The Turner and the Will Rogers Turnpikes generally parallel Route 66, but the "Free Road" remains a vital roadway, used by locals and those who avoid the tolls. The Oklahoma Turnpike Authority now operates about 600 miles of toll roads, and some 40 percent of the tolls are paid by out-of-state residents. (Oklahoma Department of Transportation.)

From 1926 to 1951, Route 66 entered Sapulpa on Old Sapulpa/ Frankoma Road. John Frank, a pottery instructor at the University of Oklahoma, founded Frankoma Pottery in 1933 and moved the business to Sapulpa in 1938. Frank died in 1973, and the family sold the business in 1991. Frankoma shut down in 2011. (Sapulpa Historical Society.)

J. Milford Davis and Otis Rule's Furniture Company erected this billboard and giant chair on Frankoma Road. After the original burned, another was built on Sapulpa Road, the new alignment of Route 66. Sapulpa was part of the land assigned to the Creek (also known as the Muscogee) Tribe, and is a Creek word meaning "sweet potato." (Sapulpa Historical Society.)

This rare structure spanning Rock Creek at Sapulpa was built in 1921 on a section of the Ozark Trails that would become Route 66. The Baltimore truss span has a brick deck with connections that were riveted rather than bolted. It is just 120 feet long by 12 feet wide and serves as the westbound gateway to one of the most scenic stretches of the Oklahoma route.

A great section of the Ozark Trails and Original Route 66 remains west of Sapulpa. East of the Rock Creek Bridge, travelers pass the ruins of Dixieland Park, which included a big swimming pool and a skating rink. It opened in 1928 and closed in 1951. The road passes under a 1925 railroad trestle before rejoining the 1952 Route 66 alignment.

This station west of Kellyville was abandoned soon after the Turner Turnpike opened in 1953. A short stretch of 1926–1938 Route 66 can still be driven nearby. It is known as the Tank Farm Loop, named for the oil tanks along the roadway. This section is listed in the National Register of Historic Places. (Oklahoma Department of Transportation.)

Bristow began as a trading post on Creek land, named for assistant postmaster general J.L. Bristow in 1901. Bristow has more miles of brick streets than any other town in Oklahoma. It was the home of Oklahoma's first radio station, KRFU, "The Voice of Oklahoma." The station became KVOO and moved to Tulsa in 1927. (Laurel Kane.)

In 1923, Lester List opened a Ford dealership at 10th and Main Streets in Bristow. Dub Bolin took over in 1959. A fire in December 2008 badly damaged the Bolin Ford dealership but spared the original building with its Model T wheel motifs on the top corners. The dealership was rebuilt in 2011 using a beautiful retro design.

Trader James W. Stroud founded Stroud as a trading post six miles from the Sac and Fox Reservation in 1892. The community thrived by smuggling whiskey to the dry reservation. Before Route 66 was commissioned, Main Street in Stroud was part of the Ozark Trails, a dirt road until 1924. (Stroud Library.)

The Skyliner Motel on Main Street in Stroud opened in 1950 and retains its classic neon sign. The 1926–1930 alignment of Route 66 turns south at the Skyliner, following State Highway 99 to Central Street. It then joins a gravel stretch of the old Ozark Trails Road and early 66 that makes 90-degree turns along the section lines.

Ed Rieves built the Rock Café in Stroud, which opened on July 4, 1939. Mamie Mayfield ran it from 1959 to 1983. Dawn Welch bought it in 1993 from Ed Smalley and has made the cafe one of the route's most popular stops. She also inspired the character Sally Carrera in the movie *Cars*. The cafe was rebuilt after being gutted by fire in 2008.

One of only seven surviving obelisks erected to mark the Ozark Trails still stands, usually covered with graffiti, on the 1926–1930 alignment southwest of Stroud. A historical steel truss bridge over Dosie Creek was about a mile to the west. Built in 1917, the bridge was probably the oldest still in use on Route 66 when it was replaced in 2004.

Joe Gibson operated Gibson's Court in Chandler, which was located close to the railroad station. Joe originally advertised 15 rooms and apartments, "all with private baths except two." The units in back were built atop private garages. Gibson's was grossing $1,100 to $1,200 per month when Joe sold in August 1945.

Joe Gibson decided to take advantage of the Route 66 traffic in 1939 and opened another motel on the east side of Chandler, the Lincoln Courts. The motel consists of two rows of redwood cabins with two units per cabin. It is still in business today as the Lincoln Court Motel. The Oklahoma Route 66 Association recently repainted the sign.

Chandler, the seat of Lincoln County, was named for assistant interior secretary George Chandler and is one of two Oklahoma cities settled by its own land run. Legendary lawman Bill Tilghman is buried in Chandler. He died in the last Wild West–style shootout at Cromwell, Oklahoma, in 1924. (Museum of Pioneer History.)

The Works Progress Administration built Chandler's native stone National Guard Armory. It sat vacant for years and was nearly demolished, but a group of dedicated locals raised money to begin restoration in 2006. The armory now houses the Route 66 Interpretive Center, an event venue, and the offices of the Oklahoma Route 66 Association. (Shellee Graham.)

John and Alice Seaba constructed this building in Warwick in 1921 as a DX station. John turned it into an engine rebuilding and machine shop and built connecting rods for the government. In 1951, he sold it to Victor Briggs, who sold to Sue and Sonny Preston in 1995. They restored the building and opened an antique shop. Today, it is the Seaba Motorcycle Museum, owned by Gerald Tims and Jerry Reis.

The notorious "Wellston Gap" remained unpaved until 1933, as state and federal officials battled over whether Route 66 would go through Wellston. Wellston and this bridge over Captain Creek ended up on a bypass, the first State Highway 66. In 1985, the "Wellston Cut-off" (the former mainline) became State Highway 66 and the route through town became State 66B.

Five

OKLAHOMA COUNTY

In 1915, Allen Threatt built a filling station at the Oklahoma/Lincoln County line, one of the first African American–owned businesses on Route 66 in Oklahoma. Now listed in the National Register of Historic Places, it stands as a testament to the fortitude of the Threatt family, who successfully operated the station during the segregation era.

Luther, near Wildhorse Creek, opened its post office in 1898 and was named for Oklahoma City businessman Luther Jones. This bridge carried Route 66 traffic over the Frisco Railroad there until 1991. The new span was built alongside the original, which was then destroyed. (Oklahoma Department of Transportation.)

This sturdy stone ruin of an old Conoco Station stands east of Arcadia. There was no electricity here, so the station used gravity fed pumps. Local lore says it closed in the 1930s after a counterfeiting operation was found in the back room. The men in the photograph are Lyle Melton (left) and Red Abbott. The site is now owned by the nearby Rock of Ages Hay Farm. (Arcadia Historical Society.)

In 1898, William H. Odor built the Round Barn at Arcadia using a design believed to be more resistant to windstorms. The burr oak timbers were soaked in water so they would bend. The landmark is shown here before its roof collapsed in 1988. Retired carpenter Luke Robison and other seniors dubbed the "Over the Hill Gang" began restoration in 1989. (Arcadia Historical Society.)

Route 66 east of Edmond was paved in brick in 1927. In 1949, it was resurfaced in asphalt and remained so until the 1980s when Arcadia Lake was constructed. The contractor acquired the original brick pavers, recognizing their potential value. The pavers now adorn at least one home in Edmond. (Oklahoma Department of Transporation.)

The tourist boom that exploded at the end of World War II was at its zenith in the mid-1950s. Many sections of Route 66 were ill equipped to handle the extra flow, and the result was slow going for those trying to get from one place to another. Here, westbound traffic tops a hill just a few miles east of Edmond. (Oklahoma Department of Transportation.)

Edward Bradbury, a former telegrapher for the Katy Railroad, operated the station at left in this photograph of the intersection of Route 66 and US 77. "Bradbury Corner" was notorious for accidents. A family named Dill operated the trading post, restaurant, and small roadside zoo in the upper right. (Oklahoma Department of Transportation.)

Camp Dixie was an early tourist camp at Edmond, advertising "comfortable cabins with garage. Cabins equipped with gas stove; sink; water piped in and out; linoleum covered floor; sanitary painted walls; clean bed linen; electric lights. Landscaping with beautiful lawn starting at $1." The site is now part of the University of Central Oklahoma.

WIDE-A-WAKE CAFE, ON HIGHWAY 66-77. EDMOND. OKLAHOMA

Originally the Night and Day Cafe, the Wide-A-Wake Cafe in Edmond was opened in October 1931 by brothers Crawford and Gene Noe along with their wives, Cleo and Essie Mae. The Wide-A-Wake had seating for 31 people and served travelers and locals until 1979. The site is now a parking lot.

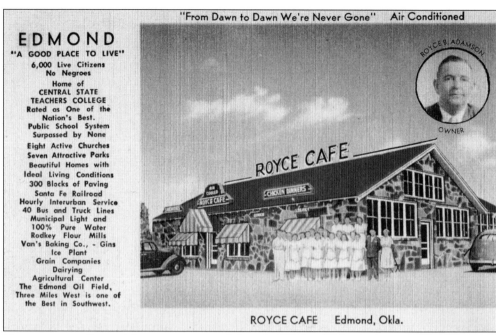

EDMOND
"A GOOD PLACE TO LIVE"
6,000 Live Citizens
No Negroes
Home of
CENTRAL STATE
TEACHERS COLLEGE
Rated as One of the
Nation's Best.
Public School System
Surpassed by None
Eight Active Churches
Seven Attractive Parks
Beautiful Homes with
Ideal Living Conditions
300 Blocks of Paving
Santa Fe Railroad
Hourly Interurban Service
40 Bus and Truck Lines
Municipal Light and
100% Pure Water
Rodkey Flour Mills
Van's Baking Co., - Gins
Ice Plant
Grain Companies
Dairying
Agricultural Center
The Edmond Oil Field,
Three Miles West is one of
the Best in Southwest.

ROYCE B. ADAMSON
OWNER

ROYCE CAFE   Edmond, Okla.

Newspaperman Royce Adamson was a good friend of Wide-a-Wake Cafe owner Crawford Noe. Adamson opened his own place in 1934, where the Knights of Columbus and Rotary Club met monthly. He touted Edmond as a "good place to live" with "No Negroes" on this postcard. The building now houses several businesses.

In 1954, Route 66 between Edmond and Oklahoma City moved to the Northeast Expressway, now Interstate 44. The $300,000 Wilshire Motel on the new route opened on August 1, 1954, and was constructed by florist and civic leader J. Wiley Richardson. It later became a halfway house for Oklahoma State Prison inmates.

In the spring of 1954, Eric Lipper opened the Clock Inn near the intersection of Eastern Avenue (now Martin Luther King Boulevard) and Route 66. The Clock Inn featured a 4,000-pound, 15-foot-wide sign with a swinging pendulum. The motel is gone, but the sign lives on at the Muscle Car Ranch in nearby Chickasha.

Jimmy Burge managed the Oklahoma Semi-Centennial celebration in 1957. He lost a bid to buy the replica oil boomtown erected for the festivities, so he built his own on Route 66. Frontier City opened on May 30, 1958, offering gunfights, train rides, and Indian dancing. Though hit hard by a tornado in 1998, the park is still going strong today.

This photograph looks east on the Northeast Expressway at Lincoln Boulevard in 1955, four years before an interchange was constructed. The work left a short section of Old 66 that was renamed Beverly Drive in honor of restaurateur Beverly Osborne, known for franchising Chicken in the Rough. (Oklahoma Department of Transportation.)

The Owl Courts were built in 1940 on the Beltline route on Britton Road. At the time, the community of Britton was not part of Oklahoma City. The office was originally a gas station, and the garages were later connected. The Owl Courts later became apartments. John Dunning bought the property and began restoration in 2004.

Executives meeting to choose a name for the new fuel developed by the Phillips Petroleum Company took note when a vehicle testing the fuel hit 66 mph on Route 66 near Tulsa. The first Phillips 66 station opened in Wichita, Kansas, in November 1927. This location was on the Route 66 Beltline in Oklahoma City. (Phillips Corporation.)

Lincoln Boulevard carried Route 66 from 1926 until 1954, bringing travelers from all points north, east, and west to the steps of the state capitol. Lincoln Boulevard had been demoted to Business Route 66 by the time this parade celebrated the widening of the showcase boulevard to six lanes in 1958. (Oklahoma Department of Transportation.)

Beginning in the 1980s, an urban renewal plan turned Lincoln Boulevard into a tree-lined thoroughfare. The plan called for demolition of the motels and other businesses, many of which had deteriorated since the construction of the interstate. The Palomino once boasted "one of the most photogenic horses in Oklahoma" out front. The Flamingo Motel was one of the last to go, demolished in 1993.

Camp Jackson was one of the first motor hotels in Oklahoma City. It opened in 1927 at 3300 North Lincoln Boulevard, nine blocks north of the state capitol. Operated by Goldie Jackson and connected to Kerr's Barbeque, it originally had 34 units. The gas station was later converted to additional units and became the Jackson Courts.

The Town House Motel, located at 3210 North Lincoln Boulevard, was constructed in 1957. Pete Grant of Oklahoma City drew up the distinctive design. The 41-unit motel that featured ultra-modern furnishings was built by Vernon Downing, city abstractor, and his partner, Joe Schmitt.

In 1953, E.C. Gentry and E.P. Roberts opened the Western Trail Motel. The motel, located at 3122 North Lincoln Boulevard, was sold to Robert Rouselle in July 1954. The sign from the motel is now displayed outside John Dunning's Western Trail Trading Post on the Beltline Route. John also owns the Owl Courts on Britton Road.

The Park-O-Tell was described as a "palace for tourists" when it opened on February 9, 1930. The complex included 68 rooms, a coffee shop, beauty parlor, a 68-car garage, and a gas station where guests could have their cars serviced while they slept. The Park-O-Tell was demolished when Lincoln Boulevard was routed around the capitol.

Beverly Osborne and his Chicken in the Rough Western girls going to the FFA and 4-H Club Live Stock Auction. It is the custom at Beverly's to buy a champion each year.

Beverly and Ruby Osborne's first restaurant was at 209 West Grand Boulevard. Their second location, on Route 66, is shown here. During a trip west in 1936, their car hit a bump as Beverly tried to enjoy her fried chicken lunch. She is said to have exclaimed, "This is really chicken in the rough." Soon, Beverly's was offering half a fried chicken with shoestring potatoes, rolls, and honey for 50¢. The meal was eaten without utensils, a novel idea at the time.

Beverley's Chicken in the Rough became one of the first franchised foods, with 250 franchises around the world. There were eight Beverly's Restaurants in Oklahoma City. The Route 66 location could seat 1,000 people, but was torn down in 1961. Beverly's Pancake House is the last survivor, now located in the Midland Center.

The Unassigned Lands of the Indian Territory opened for settlement at noon on April 22, 1889. By sunset, 4,000 people had settled on the site that became Oklahoma City. The capitol was moved from Guthrie in 1910 and housed in a hotel until this structure was ready in 1917. There was no money for a dome at the time, but one was added in 2002. (Oklahoma Department of Transportation.)

Originally, Lincoln Boulevard intersected 23rd Street in front of the capitol, as shown in this 1930s view. The Oklahoma State Capitol is the only one with active oil wells on the grounds. At center is a Pig Stand Restaurant, part of an early chain. The building resembling a home on the right was the McBride Clinic Emergency Hospital.

Garland P. Arrington operated Garland's Drive-In Restaurant at 22nd Street and Broadway Avenue from 1939 until 1950. This art deco structure offered inside dining or curb service with carhops dressed in sailor outfits with short skirts and white boots. Garland's slogan was "Tis the Taste that tells the Tale."

From 1926 to 1954, Route 66 turned west at the state capitol onto 23rd Street. Jean van Almen's Restaurant was apparently only in business for about a year beginning in 1929. Jean hung hunting trophies, guns, and at least one guitar from the ceiling, and on the walls, part of a "collection from the Southwest too beautiful to describe."

Ralph Stevens failed in several attempts to establish a successful restaurant before opening the Dolores at 33 NE 23rd Street on April 15, 1930. He named the restaurant after his daughter and set up parking stalls in back for drive-in service. The Dolores, known for its "Suzi-Q" fries, closed in 1974. (Delores Restaurant Collection.)

There were once six Cherry's Hamburgers locations in Oklahoma City, including one a few blocks west of the state capitol. The Oklahoma Historical Society identifies this as the Route 66 location, which was offering root beer for a nickel and 10¢ malts when this view was taken about 1949. (Oklahoma Historical Society.)

The Tower Theater opened on July 15, 1937, and showed *Super Sleuth*, starring Jack Okie and Anne Sothern. The 1,500-seat theater was the first located in Uptown. It closed in 1989. After sitting vacant for years, it was purchased by a local consortium for adaptive reuse. The neon sign has been restored.

The Citizen's State Bank opened in December 1958 at NW 23rd Street and Classen Boulevard. Designed by local architect Robert Roloff following Buckminster Fuller's geodesic design, it was the first dome made from gold-anodized aluminum. It now houses a cultural center, offices, and an art gallery in the old bank vault.

YOUR RESIDENTIAL

Cafeteria

WHERE U. S. HIGHWAY NO. 66 CROSSES THE FAMOUS
CLASSEN BOULEVARD AT TWENTY - THIRD STREET
OKLAHOMA CITY

Oklahoma City was once called the cafeteria capital of the world. In 1946, Ralph Geist and Naomi O'Mealey opened the Classen Cafeteria, known for its chicken pie. Naomi would go on to own four cafeterias of her own, and Geist would open the Lady Classen Cafeteria on May Avenue in 1954. The Classen Cafeteria closed in 1967.

A big milk bottle tops the former Milk Bottle Grocery on 2426 North Classen Boulevard. The tiny building is triangular because the streetcar line met Classen at an angle. The milk bottle, added in 1948, has always been leased separately. It has advertised Steffen's Dairy, Townley's Dairy, and now, Braum's. (Library of Congress.)

In 1957, smudge pots warned of repair work at the Classen Circle, where the original route on Classen Boulevard met the final path of Route 66 at the Northwest Expressway. During 1976, the route was moved onto a new elevated section of Interstate 44 that bypassed the congested and confusing circle. (Oklahoma Department of Transportation.)

CAMP HUTCHISON — OKLAHOMA CITY — On Highway 66, West

At 2114 NW 39th Street, Camp Hutchison advertised, "A place to get a good night's rest after a hard day's drive," as well as "all modern conveniences." It later became the Hutchison Courts. The remodeled complex still stands between Pennsylvania and Barnes Avenues, now painted blue and converted to apartments.

Flooding destroyed Lyle and Ruby Overman's motel on Route 66 west of St. Louis. In 1940, they opened the Major Court, later the Major Motel. It grew into the 75-unit Suntide Inn, dedicated by Miss Oklahoma on August 5, 1960. The Suntide Inn closed in 1967 and became the Kate Barnard Community Corrections Center.

BLOSSOM HEATH -- *Dine or Dance*
Two Ballrooms -- *Open the year 'round*
West 39 Street (Highway 66, West)

On July 4, 1924, Billy Gragg opened Blossom Heath, a plush roadhouse located outside the city limits. Artists such as Louis Armstrong played the dance spot, which weathered lawsuits, whiskey raids, and a receivership proceeding. It became a Moose Lodge in 1958 and was demolished for interchange construction in 1967.

Mr. and Mrs. C.J. Meadows replaced their small steakhouse with this modernistic structure that opened on February 3, 1951. This postcard advertised "Food at its best in bright, cheerful surroundings." The building at 3500 NW 39th St. was extensively remodled in 2000 and housed Meiki's Route 66 Restaurant until 2006. It is now the AutumnBridge Hospice.

A string of motels lined Route 66 west of the present-day Interstate 44/State Highway 74 interchange. The Matlyn Court was converted into the Arcadia Motel in 1957. The Arcadia is now a car lot that uses the original sign. A car lot also occupies the site of the adjacent Starlite Motel, using the bottom portion of that sign.

MATLYN COURT . . . U. S. 66 . . . Oklahoma City, Oklahoma

Cabin 4 at the Moderne Court, located at 3528 NW 39th Street, was the scene of the sensational murder of Elizabeth Jean Henderson of Compton, California, on January 10, 1954. Her traveling companion, Otto Loel, went to the chair exactly three years later. The motor court became the Nu-Homa Motel, which still stands as an RV Park.

Moderne Court, 3528 N.W. 39th St., Oklahoma City, Okla.

Lyle and Ruby Overman, owners of the Major Motel, constructed the Carlyle Motel after World War II. The cabins were arranged at a 45-degree angle around the office and residence in the middle due to a lack of space. The Carlyle is still in business at 3600 NW 39th Street, and the vintage sign remains.

The 66 Bowl at 3810 Northwest Expressway survived labor-related violence and an arson attempt before opening on March 28, 1959. It boasted 24 lanes and "Revolutionary Magic Circle" ball returns. The lanes fell silent on August 21, 2010. The sign was auctioned off, and the landmark was converted to an Indian grocery store.

On U. S. Highway 66   *De Luxe Courts*   Oklahoma City, Oklahoma

5500 N. W. 39th Street — Phone 9-3027

Mr. and Mrs. J.H. Powers owned and managed the 28-unit De Luxe Courts. In his *Guide Book to Highway 66*, Jack Rittenhouse mentioned it as one of the good courts on the western side of Oklahoma City. It later became the Motel Morocco, and the address was changed to 4500 NW 39th Street.

BOYER HOTEL COURT
U. S. 66—5120 N. W. 39—WH. 2-8179
OKLAHOMA CITY 12, OKLA.

Jack Rittenhouse, AAA, and Duncan Hines all recommended the Boyer Hotel Court on beautifully landscaped grounds at 5120 NW 39th Street. It changed hands several times, with owners including Mr. and Mrs. Cecil Cofer, Clyde H. Tyler, G.T. Stevens, and Orville Robinson. The restaurant was advertised as the "Home of Tender Coffee."

The Nazarene Church founded the town of Bethany in 1909, naming it after the biblical town adjoining Jerusalem. It became the new home for Oklahoma Holiness College, now Southern Nazarene University. The town fathers outlawed dancing, movies, alcohol, tobacco, and swearing. Those laws have been eased a bit, but Bethany still retains an old fashioned feel. (Steve Rider.)

The 24-unit Western Motel at 7500 NW 39th Expressway in Bethany was established in 1952 by John and Lora Diffee. They also founded the Diffee Motor Company, which is still in business today. The classic sign at the Western Motel, topped with a cowboy hat, is still there.

Six

CANADIAN, BLAINE, AND CADDO COUNTIES

Lake Overholser was constructed in 1919 to provide water to Oklahoma City and served as a seaplane base during World War II. The 748-foot-long Overholser Bridge opened in August 1925. It uses an unusual mixed truss design and was mentioned in *The Grapes of Wrath*. The span was bypassed in 1958 and refurbished in 2011.

Lakeview Courts
Member United Motor Courts

Approved AAA Courts	CAFE GOLF		BOAT RIDES	Selected By Duncan Hines

COOL IN SUMMER - FACING ONE OF OKLAHOMA'S LARGEST LAKES

8 MILES WEST OF OKLAHOMA CITY LIMITS	3 MILES WEST OF BETHANY	4 MILES EAST OF YUKON ON 66
Phone Bethany 612 and 322	TELEGRAPH	Mail Address R. 3, Box 23-A, Yukon

The Lakeview Courts, "For the Discriminating Tourist," faced Lake Overholser. The complex included 22 units with locking garages, a cafe, and a service station. Guests could enjoy boat rides on the lake and golfing facilities. The site became the Lakeview Pioneer Home in the 1940s and is now a convalescent center.

In 1949, the route through Yukon was expanded to four lanes. In this photograph, a connection between the new road and the old two-lane is under construction. This was done in a way to allow a future seamless merging with a planned divided four-lane highway, to be built between Bethany and Yukon over the next decade. (Oklahoma Department of Transportation.)

This image, facing east from the intersection with State Highway 4 at the east end of Yukon, captured the heavy traffic, a narrow bridge, and some of the signage on the original alignment of Route 66. The photograph was taken just before construction began on the divided four-lane highway in 1949. (Oklahoma Department of Transportation.)

Yukon's skyline is dominated by the Yukon's Best Flour Mill, founded in 1893 and acquired by John F. Kroutil, Frank L. Kroutil, and A.F. Dobry in 1902. The Dobry family opened their own mill (at right) in the 1930s. Yukon, the hometown of country music star Garth Brooks, hosts an annual Czech Festival. (Oklahoma Historical Society.)

The Star Courts at 925 West Main Street in Yukon were also known at one time as the 4-Star Courts. Owners Mr. and Mrs. W.C. Bryan advertised 18 beautiful units, "None Better at any Price." The complex, a couple of blocks east of Garth Brooks Boulevard/State Highway 92, is now El Dechado Apartments.

The Beacon Motel and Cafe opened about 1940 and later became the Big 8 Motel. The motel and room 117 were featured in the 1988 film *Rainman*. The sign was altered to read "Amarillo's Finest" for the movie. The sign was purchased by a private collector in 1999, and the motel became the DeLuxe Inn. It was demolished in 2005.

MOTEL CONWAY, EL RENO, OKLAHOMA

Route 66 is known for its motels shaped like wigwams, but El Reno once had a motel with a teepee on top. The Hotel Conway opened in October 1945 and was full every night for the first three years. It advertised, "Your Home Away from Home. Sleep in Comfort. All steel Simmons furniture, box spring mattresses."

The seat of Canadian County, El Reno was named after nearby Fort Reno, which was established in 1874 and housed some of the famous Buffalo Soldier black cavalry units. German POWs were held there during World War II. El Reno is also headquarters for the Cheyenne-Arapaho Tribe, and the legendary Chisholm Trail meets Route 66 here. (Oklahoma Department of Transportation.)

Hensley's Cafe was originally on Elm Street, relocating to the west when the highway was moved in 1946. The Hensley's Consumers Cafe was built on the same site after the four-lane highway was completed in 1957. A new facility was built on the Interstate in 1969, and this location closed a few years later. The vacant building still stands.

Publicity was a top priority for the US 66 Highway Association. Some dapper members posed for this publicity photograph in 1932 while promoting the Main Street of America in El Reno. From left to right are Guy Weadick, Mable Tompkins, Florence Weadick, and Charlie Tompkins. (Oklahoma Department of Transportation.)

GRACE'S MUSEUM AND CURIOS

2101 SUNSET   Watch for Stage Coach
                 West Side of El Reno   (Highway 66) EL RENO, OKLAHOMA

The Grace Museum and Curio Shop was a good old-fashioned tourist trap that opened just west of El Reno in 1954. Owner Oscar Grace put a stagecoach and a 1913 Model T out front. In addition to the two-headed calf and double-bodied lamb shown here, there were live buffalo, a big black bear, and a trained monkey.

Route 66 originally looped through Calumet and Geary to cross the South Canadian River at Bridgeport, where powerful state politician George Key had built a suspension bridge in 1921. He charged a stiff toll of $1 per car until the state bought the span in 1930. Bridgekeeper William "Whiskers" Phillips and his family are shown here at the tollhouse. (Carol Duncan Collection, Oklahoma Route 66 Museum.)

This view looks west across the "Pony bridge" over the South Canadian River, which bypassed George Key's suspension bridge. Officially the William H. Murray Bridge, it is made up of 38 Warren pony trusses. In the film *The Grapes of Wrath*, Grandpa Joad passed away beside this bridge. (Oklahoma Department of Transportation.)

At the time of its completion, the 3,944-foot-long Murray Bridge was second only to the Municipal Bridge at St. Louis as the longest on Route 66. The bridge was completed in July 1933; however, the opening was delayed due to the unfinished roadway immediately to the west. It finally opened to great fanfare on July 17, 1934. (Oklahoma Department of Transportation.)

In 1932, this washed-out stretch was under construction on the El Reno cutoff bypassing Bridgeport. On some rough stretches of Route 66 during the early years, the highway department kept mules on hand to pull vehicles from the muck. Local farmers charged a fee to remove those too impatient to wait. (Oklahoma Department of Transportation.)

Leon Little moved to the junction of Route 66 and US 281 after his station in Bridgeport was bypassed. Drafted in 1943, Leon leased the operation to E.B. Enze. Enze shrewdly closed it down and opened his own Hinton Junction Courts and Cafe, shown here. Leon and his wife, Ann, reopened their complex after the war. Interstate 40 arrived in 1962 and killed both businesses. Only ruins remain today.

Carl Ditmore's combination station and living quarters at Hydro was constructed in 1929. It became Provine Station when W.O. Waldrop took over in 1934. Carl and Lucille Hamons bought the station and adjoining motel units in 1941. The business was renamed Hamons Court, and Carl and Lucille went on to raise three children here. In 1962, Hamons Court closed after Interstate 40 opened east of Hydro. Lucille Hamons held on to the station and became beloved as the "Mother of the Mother Road." Lucille's was open until the day she died in August 2000. Rick Koch restored the station exterior and opened Lucille's Roadhouse in Weatherford as a tribute.

Seven

CUSTER AND WASHITA COUNTIES

Weatherford, named after colorful Marshall William J. Weatherford, is part of the area settled in the third Oklahoma land rush. It is the hometown of astronaut Thomas P. Stafford, honored by a museum here, and the home of Southwestern Oklahoma State University. This view looks east on Route 66 from Broadway Avenue.

The 40-unit Mark Motor Hotel 40 at 525 East Main Street in Weatherford developed into today's Best Western Mark Motor Hotel. The Mark has been upgraded and remodeled since the Route 66 era and gets good reviews from travelers. The Mark Restaurant is also still in business today. (Steve Rider.)

Glenn Wright's station opened in 1926 at 8th and Main Streets in Weatherford. This building was replaced with a more modern structure in 1960. Wright's Corner Mobil was owned by the family into the 1970s and closed in the 1990s. The building has been converted to another auto-related business. (Steve Rider.)

Mr. and Mrs. Bill Bergman operated the 22-unit Bill's Motel at 306 West Main Street. Like several businesses in Weatherford, it advertised a storm shelter on the property. The unique sign was replaced with a generic version, and the pink brick motel with green and pink trim closed in 1997. It was slated for demolition in 2011.

Westbound motorists entering Clinton angled onto this bridge on the Washita River, which was replaced in 1953 with a more modern, albeit less interesting, structure. The old bridge was then demolished, leaving bits of old concrete roadway still visible alongside the new approach. (Oklahoma Department of Transportation.)

FRISCO AVE. CLINTON OKLA.

This view faces west on Frisco Avenue, the Original Route 66 in Clinton. The final alignment used Gary Boulevard, named for Gov. Raymond Gary, who worked to make Route 66 a four-lane highway across western Oklahoma. Interstate 40 around Clinton opened in June 1970, but Route 66 remained on Gary Boulevard until the highway was decertified in 1985. At that time, Gary Boulevard became Business 40.

The Calmez Hotel was the first big hotel in Clinton. By the late 1950s, it had fallen into disrepair and was known for prostitution. The long-vacant landmark was torn down in October 2000 as part of the Frisco Center project. The gas station in this 1934 view was operated by D.C. Shamburg, who would later open Shamburg's Sporting Goods. (Steve Rider.)

CLINTON, OKLAHOMA

Chester and Gladys Clancy chose the site for their new motel because it was next to the busy Pop Hicks Restaurant. The Glancy opened in 1939 and was enlarged with a new sign in 1948. Chester and Gladys later operated motels in Oklahoma City, Weatherford, and Elk City. The Glancy was renovated in 2010 by new owners Jay and Sam Patel.

Greetings from Clinton, Oklahoma

Pop Hicks' Restaurant, shown here in 1960, was the best-known landmark on Route 66 in Clinton. Ethan "Pop" Hicks opened his restaurant on January 1, 1936, starting with a three-booth, seven-stool diner and a lean-to kitchen. Howard Nichols was operating the restaurant when it burned on August 2, 1999.

In 1963, veterinarian Walter "Doc" Mason and his wife, Velma, opened the Master Hosts Motor Hotel, which became the Best Western Trade Winds. Elvis Presley stayed in Room 215 four times while riding between Memphis and Las Vegas. Doc Mason donated the land across the street for the Route 66 Museum, operated by the State of Oklahoma.

Lumberyard owner Frank Granot built the first motel in Clinton in 1927. The Granot Lodge advertised "28 pleasant units—roomy and comfortable. Comfortable patio for guests with park and swimming pool near by." When this image was captured, the Granot Lodge was owned by Mr. and Mrs. H.H. Hininger. The lodge no longer stands.

During the Great Depression, the Works Progress Administration and other federal agencies put Clinton residents to work constructing McLain-Rogers Park. A beautiful Art Deco gate with glowing neon beckons visitors from Route 66. Many of the historic structures remain, including an outdoor amphitheatre.

The 20-unit Home on the Range Motel on 10th Street was advertised as a "Pleasant motel, well back from the Highway." It is now the Relax Inn. The Marshall Cafe, famous for chicken and steak dinners, was located in front of the motel. From 1926 to 1958, Route 66 used 10th Street, which becomes Neptune Drive south of town.

In 1937, Ralph Kobel opened the Y Service Station and Cafe at Neptune Park, where Route 66 and the connection to US 183 split. The station and cafe faded after Route 66 was relocated in 1958, and the adjoining Y Modern Cabins were torn down about 1992. The station is listed in the National Register of Historic Places.

Canute was originally known as Oak, renamed for the King of Denmark in 1899. Former cotton farmers Woodrow and Viola Peck opened the Cotton Boll Motel in Canute in 1960. Business fell off after Interstate 40 opened in 1970, and they sold the 16-unit motel in 1979. The motel is now a private residence, but the sign still stands.

Eight

BECKHAM COUNTY

Elk City appears on some early maps as Crowe or Busch because residents hoping to attract an Anheuser-Busch brewery changed the name of the post office from Crowe to Busch in 1901. A local temperance crusader led a campaign to change the post office name, and it became Elk City in 1907, named after nearby Elk Creek.

The Golden Boot Cafe in the heart of Elk City is shown here about 1948. It was originally Campbell's Steak House, "Known from Coast to Coast for Good Streaks, Chicken in the Rough and Sea Foods." Recommended by Duncan Hines, Campbell's offered "A Meal of Fine Food" for 25¢ to 65¢ in 1941.

The Grill in Elk City later became the Townhouse Restaurant at 111 West Third Street, where patrons were "welcome dressed as you are." The "popular air cooled restaurant offering a variety of good foods" was operated by Bess and B.F. Thornton. The building still stands today, but is now occupied by Heartland Medical.

THE MONAHAN'S RESTAURANT

1401 West 3rd St. • Hwy. 66 • Elk City, Oklahoma

Monahan's Restaurant at 1401 West Third Street, which featured a sign shaped like a shamrock, was recommended by Travel Tips and convenient to the motel row. The restaurant offered "delicious foods of large variety properly prepared and courteously served," along with an air-conditioned dining room. The restaurant no longer stands.

The Star Courts opened in 1940 and originally only had six units, which were later expanded to 12. Dr. Walter Andrewkowski and his wife bought it in 1951 and added a modern sign. Their postcards said the motel was owned by Mr. and Mrs. W.T. Andy and was "A Pleasant Stop You Will Always Remember."

"Where tired tourists meet good eats and good beds," the Motor Inn Courts offered 11 beautifully furnished cabins. Originally owned by Dr. and Mrs. B.O. McDaniel, it was later owned by W.B. Orr. A second story was later added, and the pumps were removed. It became the Motor Inn Motel but no longer stands. (Steve Rider.)

The view looking east on Route 66 from Garrett Street in Elk City has changed dramatically since this photograph was taken in the 1960s. All of the buildings on the left were demolished for the expansion of the Great Plains Regional Medical Center complex. The hospital grew out of one of the first managed care health plans, established for Elk City farmers in 1929.

The Flamingo Motel and Restaurant at 2000 West Third Street opened in 1961 and was operated by Ernest Bell until Mickey Brower took over in 1988. The 24-unit motel offered "hi-fi music" in an "attractive brick motel." It is still in business today as the Flamingo Inn. The restaurant became Pedro's Mexican Food.

Reese and Wanda Queenan moved their trading post from downtown Elk City to Route 66 west of town in 1948. Reese hired welder and Delaware Indian Johnny Grayfish. They created giant Kachina dolls from old oil drums and pipes, including a 14-foot-tall Kachina dubbed Myrtle. In 1990, Myrtle was restored and relocated to Elk City's National Route 66 Museum, where Wanda is the curator. (Wanda Queenan.)

Wanda and Reese Queenan are shown here inside the trading post in 1955. Reese passed away in 1962, and Wanda ran the business until 1980. The Queenans offered a big selection of quality goods made by local Cheyenne and Arapaho and regularly traveled to trade with Native Americans in Gallup, New Mexico. (Wanda Queenan.)

The prospect of ice-cold watermelon on a hot summer day was all it took for many motorists to pull over at the Elm Grove Motel and station, located between Elk City and Sayre on the first paved two-lane alignment of 66. Here, a family in typical 1950s fashions has stopped to take a breather. (Bill Webb.)

Paul and Ruby Mackey built the Sunset Motel on the east side of Sayre in 1950. They would later build the Western Motel next door. The Sunset was later owned by Oscar and Grace Dobbins, as well as Anne and Dwight Danberg. The 20-unit motel no longer stands, and the Bulldog Cafe was built on the site.

Bill Spence and Garth Russell's Standard Station opened in 1949. In this view, note that the older pumps in the foreground still have Standard Crowns on the top; however, the pumps under the sign are newer with no crowns. The station is no longer in business, but the building still stands at 612 NE Route 66.

Bill Spence and Garth Russell saw Gideon "Great Lightning" Wade and his family performing ceremonial dances at the 1965 New York World's Fair. They convinced the family to move to Sayre and open the Teepee Trading Post next to the service station. Wade was a descendent of both Sitting Bull and Black Kettle and became a chief of both the Cheyenne and Sioux tribes. (Steve Rider.)

Looking west on Main Street from Route 66 in Sayre, the Beckham County Courthouse is visible in the background. Constructed in 1911, it is featured in the montage showing the start of the Joad family's journey in *The Grapes of Wrath*. But it is shown out of geographical order, appearing before the jalopy reaches the Pony Bridge. The tower was restored in 2007.

Delta Motel, Hi-way 66, Sayre, Oklahoma

"Distinctly beautiful and modern in every respect," the Delta Motel advertised "popular prices and hospitality." Advertisements also mentioned that the Delta had storm shelters that could be used if the bombs fell. E.L. and Neida Martin owned the 17-unit motel, and the site became the uptown location of Puckett's Foods.

AAA recommended the Stardust Motel, "Sayre's Newest and Finest Motor Hotel." It was owned by Mr. and Mrs. Bill Feller at the time this image was captured and was later owned by John Shattuck. The postcard invited travelers to "enjoy home cooked meals and steaks in our fine restaurant." The motel still stands, and the restaurant is still in business.

Marvin and Gwindola Williams advertised that the Western Motel was the "newest and most modern motel in Sayre" during the 1960s. The 25-room Western Motel is still in business. It is best known for the classic sign featuring a colorful cactus and desert scene, a favorite of photographers.

Route 66 first crossed the North Fork of the Red River on a 2,600-foot-long bridge built entirely of timber as part of State Highway 3 in 1924. It is shown here after being updated with steel beams and a concrete deck on top of the original piers in 1933. The bridge was bypassed in 1958 and still stands on private property. (Steve Rider.)

Route 66 through Erick is named Roger Miller Boulevard after the hometown performer best known for the hit "King of the Road." Main Street was renamed to honor Sheb Wooley of Erick, whose big hit was "Purple People Eater." At the crossroads, the buildings were constructed with angles facing the intersection. (Steve Rider.)

The Mission Revival–style West Winds Motel in Erick opened shortly after World War II and was operated for many years by Floyd Pamplin. The West Winds is now a private residence. It is listed in the National Register of Historic Places, but the bucking bronco on the sign is fading rapidly.

Snake pits were among the most notorious of the Route 66 roadside attractions. Billie and Grafton Henderson operated carnival concessions before building a roadside zoo five miles west of Erick. After a tornado in 1965, they rebuilt and named the place Reptile Village. Reptile Village closed shortly after Interstate 40 opened in 1970.

REPTILE VILLAGE, OKLAHOMA
5 MILES WEST OF ERICK, OKLA. ON HIGHWAY 66 AND I-40

The 1910 Territorial Jail sits amid the ruins of Texola, a ghost town at the Texas border. In 1946, Jack Rittenhouse described Texola's "old section of stores which truly savor of pioneer days. They have sidewalk awnings of wood and metal, supported by posts. Old timers still lounge on the corners." Texola was once known as Texoma and Texokla.

Leaving Texola, the four lane alignment of Route 66 curves northwest to the Texas line, shown here in 1957. Note the Texas-shaped monument. Interstate 40 left this segment deserted in 1975.

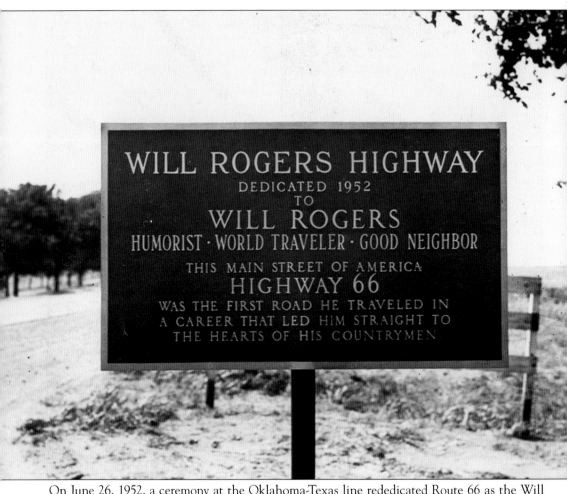

On June 26, 1952, a ceremony at the Oklahoma-Texas line rededicated Route 66 as the Will Rogers Highway. A caravan organized in part by the National US Highway 66 Association and Warner Brothers held similar ceremonies at state lines from St. Louis to Santa Monica, promoting the movie *The Will Rogers Story*. This sign disappeared, and a red granite marker was placed here in 2002. It makes a fitting place to mark the end of a journey across Oklahoma on Route 66. (Oklahoma Department of Transportation.)

After Route 66 was decertified in 1985, the Oklahoma Department of Transportation gathered 550 of the historical signs and auctioned them off in Perry, Clinton, and Muskogee. The signs, now very expensive collectibles, brought in a total of $24,000 for the highway maintenance fund. (Oklahoma Department of Transportation.)

www.arcadiapublishing.com

MAP SEARCH

Discover books about the town where you grew up, the cities where your friends and families live, the town where your parents met, or even that retirement spot you've been dreaming about. Our Web site provides history lovers with exclusive deals, advanced notification about new titles, e-mail alerts of author events, and much more.

MADE IN THE USA

Arcadia Publishing, the leading local history publisher in the United States, is committed to making history accessible and meaningful through publishing books that celebrate and preserve the heritage of America's people and places. Consistent with our mission to preserve history on a local level, this book was printed in South Carolina on American-made paper and manufactured entirely in the United States.

This book carries the accredited Forest Stewardship Council (FSC) label and is printed on 100 percent FSC-certified paper. Products carrying the FSC label are independently certified to assure consumers that they come from forests that are managed to meet the social, economic, and ecological needs of present and future generations.

FSC
Mixed Sources
Product group from well-managed forests and other controlled sources

Cert no. SW-COC-001530
www.fsc.org
© 1996 Forest Stewardship Council

Find Your Place in History.